WHISPERS OF A TEENAGER

A Collection of Short Poems

Sana Abraham

Chennai • Bangalore

CLEVER FOX PUBLISHING
Chennai, India

Published by CLEVER FOX PUBLISHING 2024
Copyright © Sana Abraham 2024

All Rights Reserved.
ISBN: 978-93-56489-47-9

This book has been published with all reasonable efforts taken to make the material error-free after the consent of the author. No part of this book shall be used, reproduced in any manner whatsoever without written permission from the author, except in the case of brief quotations embodied in critical articles and reviews.

The Author of this book is solely responsible and liable for its content including but not limited to the views, representations, descriptions, statements, information, opinions and references ["Content"]. The Content of this book shall not constitute or be construed or deemed to reflect the opinion or expression of the Publisher or Editor. Neither the Publisher nor Editor endorse or approve the Content of this book or guarantee the reliability, accuracy or completeness of the Content published herein and do not make any representations or warranties of any kind, express or implied, including but not limited to the implied warranties of merchantability, fitness for a particular purpose. The Publisher and Editor shall not be liable whatsoever for any errors, omissions, whether such errors or omissions result from negligence, accident, or any other cause or claims for loss or damages of any kind, including without limitation, indirect or consequential loss or damage arising out of use, inability to use, or about the reliability, accuracy or sufficiency of the information contained in this book.

FOREWORD

Poetry evolves from vision, imagination and inspiration. Intuition is an ingredient inseparable. Anything from God to worm, from heaven to earth, from raindrop to rainbow, from the precious to the waste, can serve as fodder. The poet who moulds is always at the helm.

Nature is the major contributor. Legends, tales and folklore supplement. The behavioural approach of man also plays an important role. Wordsworth revealed the exquisite beauty of Nature. Milton showed the ways of God to man. Keats dwelt hope and enlightened mankind. Pablo Neruda expressed solidarity with the oppressed and downtrodden.

Sana Kurian Abraham, in her 'Whispers OF A Teenager' diligently selects suitable objects as vehicle of conveyance. The poet glorifies the past rich in culture, harmony and purity, amity and unity, affection and perfection. Unflinching faith and pervading spirit of peace and tranquillity.

The poet asserts: Lies, innocent or intentional, should be shunned. Heart is the home of memories and experiences. The colour combination of the tiger is a feast to the eyes. The huge presence of pollutants threatens the very existence of the earth. Taunts and restraints of parents, though annoying, are at the bottom, aimed at correction and protection. The world should be free from blood-shed, fear and anxiety. Let there be good Samaritans all around to strengthen humanity. Withstand odds and hold on to faith. Feet at home with art, music and literature. Love books as apple of the eyes.

Sana Abraham, in her teens, blessed with the power of vision and insight, wades through the book of poetry absorbing the sights and sounds on both sides. Her mission is to enrich nature and instil the spirit of oneness and allegiana to God.

Let her dream come true. Let her fly like a butterfly fluttering up and down sucking the honey and spreading fragrance. Wish her all success.

A few lines to illustrate Sana Abraham's skill in presenting her views:

(Rainy Days)
Raindrops falling around
Like crystals falling from the sky.

(Outcry of War)
Stop the war, let the people sleep
Bring back hope, harmony and peace.

(Humanity)
When we see someone stretching out in need
When we see a heart bruised that is going to bleed
Why do we walk away blind?

(Carpe Diem)
Why do we not hear their plea?
Life is too short to sit and wait
Experience every second before it is too late

All your fears, anxieties, forget about them
Grab life by the horns and finally say carpe diem

(Anxiety)
I am staring at the stars, wishing for home
I am searching for a place that I can go.

(Faith In The Future)
Paths always change, nothing is ever the same
Keep your head up, never back away.

DR. JACOB ISAAC

www.jacobisaac.com

(Jacob Isaac is an award winning internationally acclaimed poet and scholar. His books like the Sense of Enigma, Suggestions have been recognised worldwide.

He has been awarded the Mystic Kalinga Award in 2017, the Award of Excellence in Poetry in 2017, the Sahitya Ratna Award in 2013, Michael Madhusudan Award in 2013, Honourable English Poet Award in 2014, Poetry Prize for Excellence in 2014, Best Poet of the World Award in 2013, Excellence in Poetry Award in 2011, Prestigious A Ayappan award in 2022, Royal European Doctors Literary Award, Insunation award, John Abraham award and ULPI Thailand World Congress Excellence in Poetry Award. He has also been the ambassador of Peace through Education in South Africa

Isaac was conferred the honorary Degree of Doctor of Literature in recognition of his literary contributions by the World Academy of Arts and Culture at the 34th World Congress of Poets, Peru, 2014.)

ACKNOWLEDGEMENTS

It was always my dream to be an author, and almost six years ago God made me realize that I had a talent for poetry. So, firstly would like to thank Almighty God, for giving me the talent, opportunity and an amazing support system to help me write this book. Then, I would like to thank my lovely parents: My Dad, Kurian Abraham, for being the literal backbone of this book. From researching publishers to actually producing this book, he did it all. My lovely mother, Ann Abraham for being my biggest supporter and offering me constructive criticism whenever I needed it. She always encouraged my talent for writing and is basically my media representative. So, to you both, I am eternally grateful. A small but necessary thanks to my younger brother, Shawn, though you get on my nerves, I will always love and support you. I am also thankful for my Grandparents, for the amount of love and appreciation I have received from you all. I am forever lucky to be your granddaughter. To my teachers and to my friends, a massive thanks for always pushing me to my full potential and showering me with compliments whenever I needed them.

I would like to express my deepest gratitude to Dr. Jacob Isaac Sir, who took time from his busy schedule to read my book, give feedback and write the foreword for my book. Sir, your opinion and foreword mean so much to me.

A Heartfelt thanks to Barnisha, Devika and everyone in the publishing team at Clever Fox for publishing this book, without whom this book wouldn't be a reality. I am so grateful for their efforts.

Last but not the least, my deepest gratitude is for you readers, who decided to pick up my book and give it a chance, I am forever indebted to you all for making my dreams come true!!

I sincerely hope you enjoy reading it !

INDEX

- Love 1
- Friends 2
- Lies 4
- Problems 5
- Humanity 6
- Faith in The Future 8
- The Masks of Society 10
- Enigma 12
- Anxiety 14
- Life 16
- Alone 18
- Louder than My Doubts 19
- Home 21
- They Mean More to Me 22
- Carpe Diem 24
- Outcry of War 26
- The Earth a 1000 Years Ago 27
- Serenity 29
- A Star of Hope 31
- Invisible Intruder – Covid 19 32
- Rainy Days 33
- The Tiger 35
- Pollution 36
- Reverie 37

LOVE

Why do we say that we're falling in love?

Aren't we supposed to fly?

Aren't our spirits supposed to soar like doves

Or am I aiming too high?

Is it just an elysian lie,

Way too good to be true?

Is it a feeling of lost goodbyes,

That thickens the air in a room?

But love, Oh! it is an orphic thing.

Maybe I understand why we fall,

Cause flying shows the happiness it brings,

But not the way it could kill us all.

FRIENDS

We all have various friends in our life,

Someone to talk to during our strife.

But, only after a friendship ends, do we see,

If they were just being nice or actually true to me.

I met this friend and I hated her so,

But when we talked, seeds of friendship had been sown,

Alas, when I went to her and said, "troubles I'm having, help I seek."

She said, "oh that sucks but let's get back to me."

I met another and we were thick as thieves,

But then I stumbled and she rose above me.

Envy and distrust creeped into my heart,

And slowly our conversations became further and further apart.

I was friends with two and we were close,

Shared with each other, the secrets we guarded the most.

But as time dragged on, they forgot about me,

So, every time we waved, I saw in their eyes the secrets I won't ever see.

But then there was one, since we were 8,

We laughed and bonded and became the best of mates.

Every time, to fit in, I pushed her away,

And when I got rejected, with me she always stayed.

What I mean to say, is that, friends always come and go.

Who is that special one, how can we ever know?

Maybe, we just need to go through life and see,

When a bond is formed through trust and love, that's a friend who's true to me.

LIES

Lying is bad that's what parents say

But haven't they lied till today?

Parents use lying for our own safety reasons,

Parents use lying for our own protection.

But the question is why do children lie?

Maybe they are embarrassed or just too shy?

Maybe they are nervous tensed or worried,

Or they just think that the secret shoudn't be hurried.

Lying is bad, mean mean and sad

If you have tried it never be glad.

You should never be proud if you lied anyway,

Cause lying is bad any day.

PROBLEMS

I have problems too,

And I am left wondering what to do?

It could be about my brother annoying me the whole day,

Or my parents telling me to study instead of play.

It could be about losing a friend,

Or my teacher shouting at me when I think it's the end.

It could be about some homework or about school,

And sometimes I am left wondering whether I was a fool?

And then I calm down and I realize,

Something I have never seen, I do have people, people to help me,

I find out that I am not alone,

I have parents that comfort me when I am torn.

I also have very good friends,

Whose help and support I have till the very end.

HUMANITY

When we see someone stretching out in need

When we see a heart, bruised that's going to bleed,

Why do we walk away blind?

Why do we not hear their plea?

Why have we been trained to say no?

Just because it does not affect us so,

When other's suffering we seem to miss,

In that case, is ignorance really bliss?

Why do we put on a show?

When we die, to the same place don't we all go?

Why do we choose to be apart?

Is being emphatic really that hard?

Just lend out a hand,

Raise others up so that they may so also stand.

Help them fix their heart's broken pieces,

Let them know what love really is

It's not very hard to acknowledge someone's existence

Please don't keep others at a distance

Once just give it a try

You could have, at that moment, changed someone's life!

Why carry around this false sense of vanity?

Spread Love, Peace, Hope,

Let people know that this is Humanity.

FAITH IN THE FUTURE

The world is filled with un-sureties,

Each little bubble of doubt darkens our clarity,

When the time ahead seems bleak,

Faith in the future we must keep.

Life may cause you to stumble,

When the walls, you built so high starts to crumble,

When you see your hope diminish and die,

Keep Faith in the future held up high.

Paths always change; nothing is ever the same,

Keep your head up never back away!

When worry and panic seems to dawn,

Let your Faith in the future be strong.

Predicaments and turmoil seem to drag on, however

Remember these troubles have the shortest forever.

Soon you'll stand up strong, brave and take things with a bit of humour,

All because you kept faith in the future.

THE MASKS OF SOCIETY

Looking at a mirror, and all the broken shards,

Couldn't hide the person behind the false façade.

The masks of laughter and smiles,

Can never cover the pains of the human mind.

All those short conversations, probably filled with lies,

Thwarted the attention from the true thoughts inside.

Mere objects are used to cover up human beauty,

Just to be accepted in this miniscule society.

Built on failure and broken trust

The inner being, covered by walls, stayed there, catching dust.

And if a crack on that wall ever did appear?

Anger and rage stitched up that tear.

Why have we come to this?

A society full of false bliss.

Let your true self come bursting out,

Show yourself without a doubt.

A diamond in the rough, you shall be,

A tremendous yes in a room full of maybes.

You can finally let down your guard

Cause ignore the world, and let yourself be who you are!

ENIGMA

Who is the enigma that lives in my brain?

Judging what I do every single day?

She tells me to act with reason,

Or sometimes I act impulsively, depending on what mood she's in.

She tries to make me feel insecure and unloved,

And sometimes to her, I tend to succumb.

She's like the omniscient narrator in my life,

Every move I make, she does always analyze.

She sets out to watch me break,

Reminding me of all the mistakes I make.

She's the reason I lie awake at night,

Wondering, if like the stars, I could ever shine so bright?

Who is she, to tell me so?

Preventing me to spread my wings and soar?

Why do I let her influence who I am?

Why is she the shepherd and me the lamb?

Doesn't she live in my own mind?

So, can't I push her somewhere I can't find?

I won't let her voice have the last say,

She can't tell me what all I have to change.

I have to be in control now,

Right here with my people around.

When she does resurface in my brain,

I will be the first to tell her that she'll never be a part of me again!

ANXIETY

I'm Running AND Running, I'm Running Out OF Time

I'm Chasing, I'm CHASING Something That Isn't Mine

I'm Falling, I'm Falling, I'm Falling Behind

I'm Going I'm Going TO A Place That I Can't Find

Who Am I Who Am I

And I Don't Know Myself

Where Am I Where Am I

I'm Lost AND I Need Help

I Look Around AND The World Goes Up IN Smoke

I Look Around AT A Place that I Don't Know

I'm Staring AT The Stars, Wishing FOR Home

I'm Searching FOR A Place That I Can Go

Who Am I Who Am I

And I Don't Know My Self

Where Am I Where Am I

I've Created My Own Hell

I'm Breaking, I'm Drowning, I'm Sinking IN My Own Sea

I'm Shaking, I'm Not Breathing, What Else Could I Be

I Can't Ever Know

I Can't Ever Show

I Can Never Let Go

Of Who I'm Supposed TO Be

LIFE

Isn't it funny how the world works?

People say something, then completely differ.

Life does give the twists and turns and the occasional jerks,

It's never what you thought or what you'd prefer.

We spent our childhood fantasizing about the future,

Now we spend our present dreaming about the past,

But does anyone realize that it is through hardships that we were nurtured,

And gave us memories that will last.

We might have lost our best friend forever,

Cause forever isn't what it always seems,

But because of that bond you shared together,

You'll still be a part of each other's stories.

Yeah, so maybe life's not what I thought it would be,

It was always a rollercoaster of emotions and changes of plans,

So, I'll accept that change is life's only guarantee,

Cause this change is what made me who I am!

ALONE

Feeling closed behind a fake door,

Being held by invisible chains,

Don't know what to do anymore,

Wondering whether you will live again.

It's a losing battle,

With no one on your side,

It's all a mind game,

And you don't want to fight.

Feeling empty and soulless,

Pondering where did God go?

Enveloped by darkness's shadow.

But somewhere you see a light,

A ray of shinning hope.

Feeling happy, feeling bright,

A feeling you lost long ago.

This helping hand is all you sought,

Soon you feel loved and you don't feel weak.

A crown of safety and joy you adorn

Cause now you know you aren't alone

LOUDER THAN MY DOUBTS

I feel like I'm sinking inside a sea full of my doubts,

Running in a circle with no way out,

Not sure where I'm supposed to go?

Like every path I take brings me back to point zero.

Which direction should I take?

What all choices do I make?

I feel like my own foe,

Should I make my own path or find someone else's to follow?

A million voices in my head,

Keep me awake as I lie in my bed.

Maybe, if I did something sooner,

I would have been sure of my future?

When the people in my head get too loud,

I look back on what I did to be where I am now.

I'll try to march to the beat of my own drum,

Feeling proud of how far I've come.

If I could I wouldn't change anything now,

Thankful to the people, who sacrificed everything to show me how.

If I'm scared, I know I'll let them down.

so, I swear, I won't let my insecurities drown me out

and I will rise higher and be louder than my doubts.

HOME

Home is where the heart is.

Whatever does that mean?

Could it be a place or a person maybe?

A home is a thing that makes you feel safe,

It could be a person you confide in or chilling in your house midday,

A home could be a special place where you make precious memories

Or a person with whom you experience all of your stories.

A home is where your troubles go away,

A person who, during all your stresses with you always stays.

So wherever or with whomever your heart just never wants to leave,

That is your real home, its true believe me.

THEY MEAN MORE TO ME

Wonderful places I could go,

Sitting at home on my bedroom floor.

A melody of music it may be,

But it means so much more to me.

A home for my heart and life to my mind,

Each note has hidden treasures for me to find.

A melody of music it may be,

But it means so much more to me.

People, creatures I would have never known,

Conversations that make me wiser so.

A bundle of paper it may be,

But it means so much more to me.

Music, art, books, these things they shine,

Like they are the apple of my eye.

To you, of no value, they may be,

But they all mean so much more to me.

CARPE DIEM

By each passing moment, the days fly past,

It makes us want them more, but they won't last.

The times where we should be happy, we shed a tear,

We were fuming while others spread cheer.

The moments with people we will never see again,

Now all we have left are some souvenirs in our brains.

All in a hurry to grow up, So many dreams, so many plans,

Now I wish I had taken it all in when I had the chance,

When life passes by we'll probably go our separate ways,

But we will always regret never enjoying the good old days!

So if there is a moment, it could be just a flicker,

Seize it, grab it, never let it disappear.

Life's too short to sit and wait,

Experience every second before it's too late.

All your fears, anxieties, forget about them,

Grab life by the horns and finally say, CARPE DIEM.

OUTCRY OF WAR

Blood, Bodies everywhere.

Why can't two nations never be friends?

All they care about is Money, Land and Superiority,

Why can't Human lives be your priority?

For all the people who got caught in the crossfire,

Their livers are oh so very dire.

Stop the war, save all these lives,

Let people come back to their children and wives

Stop the war, give the people a break from the fear,

Let them know that loved ones are here

Stop the war, let the people sleep

Bring back hope, harmony and Peace.

THE EARTH A 1000 YEARS AGO

Do you know what the world was like a 1000 years ago?

There was no coughing or sneezing from breathing all this smoke,

The water sparkled, the birds sang,

All animals had homes, butterflies had flowers to land.

The trees grew big and strong,

But us humans, felt that this was wrong,

We wanted more technology,

To become an advanced race was our aim,

Did we notice that because of us what the earth became?

Ashy clouds filled the sky, and waters turned green,

So many species never again to be seen.

The trees fell down to become our homes,

Now birds and animals wonder where did theirs go?

So let's try to restore the earth, back to a 1000 years ago

Where the icebergs will still be there and global warming will be no more,

Fishes swimming happily with no plastic for them to choke,

Animals can move freely, with water left for them in which they can soak.

Let's do it so our future generation can live in a beautiful world

The way God had designed it so,

And they will never have to wonder about the earth a 1000 years ago

SERENITY

The clouds were of various shapes oh, so very high,

The eagles wove in and out of them, soaring in the crystal sky.

All the trees danced as the wind made it's way,

Even the smallest blade of grass started to gently sway.

The roses, bluebells and lilies, exhibited their colours, red, blue and white,

The dew drops on them glistened, when the sun shone it's light.

I heard the chattering of the children, playing on the ground,

And the several different kinds of birds, made a cacophony of sounds.

I look out of my balcony at a sight of pure bliss,

The waves crashing on a nearby shore, produces a silent hiss.

Sometimes there's a scent of petrichor that lingers around me,

Or the scent of freshly bloomed flowers, growing on the trees.

When I close my eyes and sit outside, I'm in such a peaceful state,

And when I open them their beauty brings a smile to my face.

In this very second, I worry not of my future or my past,

But how I wish, I could freeze this moment, so that forever it could last.

A STAR OF HOPE

As a child I looked to the sky,

At the stars up, so high.

And chose the one that shone so bright,

Claimed it, took it and made it mine.

I made a wish everyday,

Thought it would show me the way,

New, new things I would ask and say,

As if it would grnat it them from a billion miles away.

Even though now ,I don't know if they will come true?

I'm glad I kept that hope, to look up to.

Cause no matter how old I get, when I'm feeling blue,

I look up at the stars and hope my wishes come true.

INVISIBLE INTRUDER – COVID 19

The Streets are empty, no crowds at all,

Everyone's at their houses, no one is coming out, no one at all!

Though the sun shines bright, we don't know if it is safe,

As there are viruses in the air and for the victims it waits.

Cough and Sneezes are its private jets

And our precious lungs it affects.

All our frontline workers are superheroes, masks and sanitizers are our friends,

We must take safety precautions to prevent our end.

Nevertheless, plants are growing green and pollution is amiss,

The water is back to clear, Nature is once again bliss.

So, I am happy I'm home with my family around,

I'm glad God is keeping all of us safe and sound.

RAINY DAYS

Raindrops falling all around,

Feels like crystals falling from the sky.

Seldom when the sunlight peeps,

We can see a rainbow up on high.

People sitting in their homes,

Snug with a bowl of soup.

Children splashing in puddles,

Covering themselves with mud and goop.

The snakes and frogs and toads come out,

And sit on the porch all day.

The storms, thunder or the lightning,

Does not scare them away!

When the lights go out,

We all sit near the candlelight.

Playing Uno, Charades and other games,

Just to pass the time.

All the wet and messy fun!

And the different things we play,

No more heat and dust,

Makes me love these rainy days!

THE TIGER

If I had a favorite animal,

A tiger it would be.

The way it has slender, black streaks

On its orange, gleaming body.

Every night it looks for gore,

May be a deer, a horse or a wild boar.

Tigers can be creatures full of love and benevolence,

We hurt these poor creatures to put trophies on our shelves.

Let's revive them and bring them to life!

If I had a favorite animal,

A tiger it would be,

As it is beautiful and majestic for us to see!

POLLUTION

The Earth's Pollution

Will lead to our destruction.

About fame and success is all you care

But don't you care about the Earth's welfare?

We are the trouble,

Why the Earth's heating upon the double.

Wastage and Plastic,

That is our planning

But for the earth is it nice?

Think about it twice.

Pollution, Overpopulation and Global Warming,

Which for us is a very big warning!

So, a helping hand let us lend

To save our earth from its end.

REVERIE

The sun shone on the crimson flowers,

The dew drops dressed the spiderwebs,

Over the grass, the insects hover,

The birds hopped on their legs.

The smell of petrichor enveloped us all,

The sound of laughter filled our ears,

Oh, weren't just we having a ball,

Living without fear?

But as the years flew by, our visages creased,

Not due to the passage of time,

But because our worry grew not ceased,

Depriving our eyes of their shine.

Alas! when those rare moment come by,

Allowing us to reminisce,

Our faces bend into a ghost of a smile,

Oh, how those days do I miss!

www.ingramcontent.com/pod-product-compliance
Lightning Source LLC
LaVergne TN
LVHW041641070526
838199LV00052B/3487